Australian Biographical Monographs

1

# Joseph Lyons
## and the management of adversity

## Kevin Andrews

Connor Court Publishing

Published in 2016 by Connor Court Publishing Pty Ltd

Copyright © Kevin Andrews 2016

All rights reserved. No part of this book may be reproduced or transmitted in any form or by any means, electronic or mechanical, including photocopying, recording or by any information storage and retrieval system, without prior permission in writing from the publisher.

Connor Court Publishing Pty Ltd
PO Box 7257
Redland Bay QLD 4165
sales@connorcourt.com
www.connorcourt.com
Phone  0497-900-685

Printed in Australia

ISBN: 978-1-925501-33-9

Front cover design:  Maria Giordano
Front cover picture: Portrait of Joseph Aloysius Lyons [picture].
http://nla.gov.au/nla.obj-136265031

"We must put our house in order. I know that it is unpopular to talk about cutting down expenses, but we have to do it."

- Joseph Lyons, March 13, 1931

# Contents

| | | |
|---|---|---|
| 1. | Introduction | 9 |
| 2. | Adversity and Opportunity | 13 |
| 3. | Management of Debt | 27 |
| 4. | Turbulent Times | 39 |
| 5. | Saving the Nation | 61 |
| 6. | Public Leadership | 77 |
| 7. | Select Bibliography | 83 |

# 1

# Introduction

This monograph was originally delivered as the 36th Daniel Mannix Memorial Lecture for the Newman College Students' Club at the University of Melbourne on September 7, 2016. The lecture series was founded by Francis Moore, Nicholas Green and me in 1977 when we were students at Newman. Our intention was to mark the 60th anniversary of the ascension of Daniel Mannix as Archbishop of Melbourne by initiating a series of lectures to examine the art and science of public leadership. Our purpose was to honour the leadership of Mannix in founding Newman College. It was at the opening of Newman in 1918 that Mannix remarked:

> My hope for the future is very largely centred in Newman College, and in that band of students who will pass through its walls year after year. You are the first of that band . . . in whom the hope of the Catholic Church – and indeed the hope of Australia is most firmly fixed.

In choosing Mr BA Santamaria to speak about Mannix in the inaugural lecture, we hoped to set a pattern of a person prominent in a profession, vocation or calling reflecting on another person with whom they had been associated or who had also been a leader in that walk of life. We anticipated that such reflection would help to illuminate the art and science of public leadership in Australia. Hence the early lectures: BA Santamaria on Archbishop Mannix, Sir Zelman Cowen on Sir Isaac Isaacs, Sir Paul Hasluck on Sir Robert Menzies, and Sir Bernard Callinan on Sir John Monash.

My choice of subject – Joseph Aloysius Lyons, the 14th Prime Minister of Australia (and the tenth person to be elected to that office) – sought to honour the original intention of the Newman College Students' Club.

The sub-title of the lecture - the management of adversity – is significant. In my participation in public life for more than a quarter of a century, and my close observation of Australian political leaders, including seven Prime Ministers, I have concluded that it is not the grand rhetorical gestures, the proclamation of aspirations, or even the implementation of proposals and policies that mark the true measure of a leader, but the response to the unexpected, the unwanted, and the unanticipated events that arise. In other words, it is the management of crises, not the projection of aspirations, which is the true mark of leadership.

History is shaped by crises and unexpected events. Leadership is determined by the response to them. Truly great leaders are those who have risen successfully to the unanticipated challenges. Poor leaders are those who pretend to themselves, and seek to convince others, that the crises or challenges do not exist.

Like previous lecturers in the Mannix Memorial Lectures, I sought to explore the contribution of Joseph Lyons to the art and science of public leadership in Australia.

# 2

# Adversity and Opportunity

The fifth child of Michael and Ellen Lyons, Joseph was born at Stanley in northern Tasmania in September 1879. The young Joe appeared to have experienced relatively carefree early years in the company of his older brothers and sisters, first at Stanley and later at Ulverstone where his family moved when he was about five years old. At the age of nine, however, he had to leave St Joseph's Convent School, Ulverstone to help support the family after his hardworking and relatively prosperous father lost the family's finances gambling on the 1887 Melbourne Cup. Fortunately for the young Joe, two aunts supported him to return to school at Stanley at age 12, where under the guidance of a sympathetic teacher, John Scott, he completed his education, became a paid monitor of younger pupils, and eventually a teacher at various country schools and a graduate of

Tasmania's first teacher's college.

It was during his time as a teacher in small rural schools that Lyons helped found the North-West branch of the Worker's Political League, the forerunner of the Labor Party in Tasmania. At first a tentative public speaker, Lyons gained confidence as his engaging, plain-speaking style emerged during many union and public meetings.

Some of the formative influences on Lyons remained throughout his life, especially his concern about personal finances and the need to provide for his family, both as a child and later as a married man. His wife, Enid, recalled that 'the hardships of his childhood and the struggles of his youth . . . helped to make him the politician and man he was.' He was in correspondence about his salary on numerous occasions with the Director of Education, with whom he would also clash about the right of public servants to engage in political activities. On two occasions, when in Opposition in the Tasmanian Parliament, Lyons commenced a business to supplement his income, and as Opposition Leader, commenced articles of clerkship to improve his professional qualifications. Indeed Lyons' complaints about his salary level became an issue in the State Parliament which elevated the prominence of the young teacher in Labor circles.

The unique situation of Tasmania amongst the Australian states afforded Joe Lyons opportunities that may not have occurred elsewhere. With a small population – of less than 200,000 people in 1910 – and the absence of a significant mining and manufacturing base, the Teachers' Association became a major vehicle of Labor influence and opposition to the then Nationalist Party government of Premier John Evans. The west coast mining boom, commemorated in Geoffrey Blainey's history, *The Peaks of Lyell*, was isolated from Hobart, and employed relatively few people by the early decades of the 20$^{th}$ century. With manufacturing smaller than on the mainland, union influence did not flourish to the same extent in Tasmania. The Australian Workers Union, for example, was not established on the island until 1909, two decades after its origins in Queensland.

Concerns about his income falling – from £125 to £100 per annum – and re-employment prospects as a teacher were a significant consideration in Lyons' hesitancy to stand for public office at the 1909 Tasmanian election despite his growing involvement in the fledgling State Labor movement. On the first occasion at which the Hare-Clarke voting system was used, the short campaign required the candidates in just five State electorates to travel long distances, often over barely formed roads, to the many villages and hamlets that comprised the constituency of Wilmot in Tasmania's north. Lyons had previously journeyed through much of the State to speak on Labor movement platforms, and his frequent travelling and attentiveness to the electorate would remain a pattern of his political life, even when Premier of Tasmania and, subsequently, Prime Minister of Australia.

Lyons placed third of the six successful candidates in the electorate, beginning a significant contribution to public life in Australia as the representative of the people of Wilmot in the State and Commonwealth Parliaments for the following three decades. Little did anyone know that the slightly plump, medium height 30 year-old with a distinctive patch of curly black hair making his Maiden Speech in the Tasmanian House of Assembly in 1909 would become Premier of the State, Prime Minister of Australia and one of the most well-known and liked public figures in the first half of the 20th century.

The themes that Joseph Lyons developed in his campaign and in that first speech were a constant throughout his public life: concern for ordinary Australians, the worker, women and the challenges to the development of his State. In modern political parlance, his concerns were for families, jobs and growth.

In her Maiden Speech, upon being the first woman elected to the House of Representatives in 1943,

Enid Lyons encapsulated her late husband's political concerns when she said:

> I bear the name of one of whom it was said in this chamber that to him the problems of government were not problems of blue books, not problems of statistics, but problems of human values, human hearts and human feelings.

Apart from two years from 1914-16, when he served as Deputy Premier, Treasurer, and Minister for Railways and Education in Tasmania's initial Labor government, following the resignation of the Nationalist administration, Lyons' first decade and a half was spent in Opposition. It was a period of considerable national ferment during which many of the enduring fault lines in the Australian polity were revealed. The early decades of the new Commonwealth of Australia witnessed the rise of socialism and Fabianism within the Labor movement; the disruption of the Great War and the bitterness of the conscription debates; and the divide over protection and free trade which led to the uneasy arrival at the subsequently named 'Australian Settlement' since defined by the leading journalist and author, Paul Kelly, as Industrial Arbitration, Industry Protection, a White Australia, State Paternalism and Imperial Benevolence.

Lyons' positions on many these issues have given

rise to some of the subsequent criticisms of him, but they were more nuanced than some critics have liked to paint. An example was his approach to arbitration and protection. Lyons political education had begun whilst he was a student at the Tasmanian Teachers College where he joined a Fabian discussion group at the Denison Branch of the Labor Party. There he met Lyndhurst Giblin, subsequently a colleague in the Tasmanian Parliament and an economist who was to have a significant influence on Lyons throughout his public life. Through the second decade of the $20^{th}$ century, Lyons promoted a socialist ideal against the failures of capitalism with increasing frequency and zeal, leading the Nationalist Party Premier, Walter Lee, to assert in 1921 that Lyons 'favoured revolution by the destruction of the capitalist system.'

Lyons' apparent fervour should be viewed in the context of both the times and Tasmania. Speeches rallying the workers, or appealing to fellow travellers do not necessarily reflect the subtleties of a political philosophy. As his biographer, Anne Henderson, observes,

> Lyons' support for the Labor ethic of a better deal for the working classes and a widening of state responsibility was instinctive. He was not immersed in the tracts of the Fabians or in Marxist traditions, although he did call himself a socialist and addressed his colleagues in the tribal leftist way as 'brother' or 'comrade'.

The Labor movement in Tasmania charted a more moderate course than elsewhere in Australia, partly in response to isolation, partly a reflection of small communities in which employers and employees had closer relationships, and partly an acknowledgement that solutions devised on the mainland had to be modified for local conditions. This was particularly the case when Lyons became Premier in 1923. The famous *Harvester* decision of 1907 had established a minimum wage for workers, but in doing so, it also created what one of the leading economists of the era, Douglas Copland, described as the most rigid economy in the world. The *Report of the Committee Appointed to Inquire into Tasmanian Disabilities Under Federation,* which had been established by Lyons as Premier in 1925, concluded that the *Navigation Act,* and the Federal Court of Arbitration, both of which adversely affected the State because of the high cost of labour; and the protective tariff and free trade between the states combined to constrain economic activity and employment on the Island. As Anne Henderson observes, upon becoming Premier and having to address the challenges facing his State, 'much of the radicalism in Lyons' rhetoric during his opposition would disappear.'

Another example of Lyons' more pragmatic instinct relates to what Paul Kelly entitled 'Imperial Benevolence'. Here I include both the role of the

Crown and the Empire.

No issue since Federation has caused as much political turmoil in Australia as the conscription debates during the First World War. Neither the Vietnam War nor the Whitlam Government dismissal, two divisive events of more recent times, generated the bitter passions that erupted in 1916 and 1917 when Labor Prime Minister Billy Hughes proposed to introduce military conscription. A pacifist, Joseph Lyons opposed conscription, but supported Australia's involvement in the Great War. Unlike Archbishop Mannix, after whom this lecture series is named, Lyons did not regard the European conflict as a trade war. He supported the Empire but opposed conscription. He was mindful also that Britain had not offered any compensation to Australia for its efforts in a faraway conflict.

The Great War also exposed an undercurrent of ugly sectarianism in Australia which was exacerbated by the conflation of the troubles in Ireland and the war against Germany. In 1913, the Irish Home Rule Bill had passed the House of Commons three times, overcoming the constitutional block of the House of Lords, but it was effectively ignored by British military forces in Ireland and the Asquith government, leading to the Easter Rising of 1916 and the subsequent execution of its leaders. For many Irish nationalists in Australia, respect for English constitutionality was shattered.

Archbishop Mannix had played no real part in the 1916 conscription referendum, which was lost, but was drawn into the 1917 debate, after he stated that he believed Australia was doing as much as it should in the European war. Billy Hughes seized upon the Mannix statement to establish a sectarian issue about which he could rally support for his second attempt to introduce conscription.

As Mr Santamaria pointed out in the inaugural 1977 lecture, Dr H V Evatt in his book *Australian Labour Leader,* a biography of the NSW Premier William Holman, and a supporter of Hughes, set out the strategy of the 'little digger':

> Mr Hughes made his fight definitely an anti-Mannix fight, as a matter of tactics. Mannix, he said, is against the British Empire. Very well, then, we are against Mannix. At one time it looked as if the whole organisation of the campaign was very much less concerned with the defeat of the Hun than with that of the turbulent Catholic prelate.

Mannix was not opposed to conscription itself: indeed he was silent on the issue during the Second World War. His issue was with the extent of Australia's participation. Hughes unleashed a torrent of sectarianism that swept the nation. Large rallies across Australia often erupted into chaos and violence. Speakers were the target of physical attack, including Joseph Lyons in Tasmania. My father, who was born into an Anglican family in 1911, recalled the bitter divisions and recriminations in a small Victorian country town during his childhood.

People of German heritage were rounded up and detained. German place names were changed. Hence in my electorate, Wilhelm and Bismark Streets, and German Lane were renamed King, Victoria and George Streets. The fact that these original street names had been chosen by Lutherans who settled in Australia after escaping Prussia's rising militarism from the 1860s was lost in the fervour of the times.

The issue split the Labor Party nationally. In November 1916, two weeks after losing the first conscription vote, Billy Hughes walked out of the Labor Party caucus, taking 23 supporters with him. With support from the Liberals, Hughes formed a new Nationalist government. The following May, he won the 1917 election and subsequently introduced the second conscription referendum. So determined was Hughes to pass the proposal that he censored the 'no' case. Despite this, the proposal was lost by a larger margin than the first referendum. News of the horror of the Great War was slowly reaching distant Australia. A century ago on the Somme, at Fromelles and Pozieres, thousands of young Australians were killed within hours in bombardments and bloody trench warfare. Even a majority of Australians on active service voted against the second conscription proposal, a reversal of their position just a year previously.

Although the 1917 referendum failed nationally, a majority of Tasmanians voted in favour of conscription, as they had in 1916. The bitter recriminations continued during the war years as support for the Irish cause was seized upon by some groups as opposition to the British in the conflict against Germany. Despite being supported by a majority of Tasmanians, the Labor leader, John Earle, was replaced by caucus with the pacifist Lyons soon after the first 1916 vote. Earle accused Lyons of exploiting the situation for his political advantage, but there was little sympathy for Earle amongst his colleagues after having campaigned to traditional Labor voters with the conservatives in favour of conscription.

There was little political advantage for Lyons in opposing conscription, as the inhabitants of the island state, conservative in nature, rallied to Hughes' clarion call again in 1917. Lyons position on the issue had deeply personal consequences. Friendships were broken. Hughes played the sectarian card even though Catholics were not united on the conscription issue. People of integrity and good will stood on different sides of the fence. A number of bishops had supported compulsory enlistment, the Vatican Secretariat of State had urged Mannix to modify his public activities, and a personal friend of Joe Lyons, Fr Tom O'Donnell, who had officiated at his wedding to Enid in 1915 had campaigned for conscription throughout Tasmania, leading to their estrangement.

The conscription debates highlight an aspect of Lyons' character that was evident at critical points of his public life: the preparedness to place principle above populism; and the rejection of the sectarian in favour of a common humanity. On becoming Opposition leader in 1916, Lyons said:

> It may be conceded that the present division may throw the party back temporarily in a parliamentary sense but . . . it has always seemed to me that the solidarity of the Labor Party and its fidelity to principle is a much more important matter than the mere numbers of the party in parliament.

The tenor of the statement suggests a more ideological Lyons than subsequent history records. It may be, as his biographer, Anne Henderson records, by 1923 when he became Premier, he had realised that 'solidarity is all very well, but a parliamentary leader should be destined also to govern.'

Lyons' Catholicism did not define his political

views. He had supported Irish Home Rule, and at one stage, advocated the abolition of the State Governor and the Legislative Council, but supported King and Empire. He opposed sectarianism, even leading a debate in the House of Assembly about scurrilous pamphlets that had been distributed in the state by the Loyalty League, but rejected the campaign by the Catholic Federation for state aid to religious schools, even blaming the group for a decline in his vote at the 1919 elections. Yet he was an honorary member of the St Vincent de Paul Society.

According to Anne Henderson:

> Lyons had little faith in sectional interest groups to make a political difference without their inclusion in the mainstream. He also sensed the fragility of social cohesion and the potential damage from any outbreak of militant sectarianism in a strongly Anglo-Protestant dominance of a minority Irish Catholic tradition. His mother's interest in Irish politics had familiarised Lyons from an early age with the history of such protest.

# 3

# Management of Debt

The one constant in the public leadership of Joseph Lyons was the management of debt. From the outset of his parliamentary career in Tasmania, he spoke about the challenges of state debt and the cost of repaying it. When Lyons first became State Treasurer in 1914, his friend and colleague, Lyndhurst Giblin, later to become one of the foremost economists in Australia, was a significant influence. The message which Lyons absorbed – and which was to remain his political credo throughout his public life – was that unproductive debt was a drain on the economy through higher interest payments and higher taxes that ultimately fell upon workers. With a small population, Tasmania was particularly affected.

In 1915, Lyons established a Royal Commission into Public Debts and Sinking Fund to examine a sinking fund for state debt as a counter to profligate government. Preceding a Future Fund by decades, the idea failed to mature as the nation's financial challenges were compounded by the cost of the Great War.

Tasmania faced increasingly critical challenges. By the early 1920s, the isolated island state was suffering from a stagnating economy and widespread emigration of workers and families to the mainland. The seeds of the Great Depression were already growing, as the economic historian, CB Shedvin observed:

> The economy stagnated: real national product fell gradually, and product per head more rapidly, so that by 1927 – well before the overseas collapse – Australia was already in a state of serious recession.

By 1922, Tasmania was paying a third of its revenue in interest on debts. The Labor newspaper, *The World*, estimated when Lyons came to power in 1923, that half of the government's revenue was being paid in interest. The new Premier was confronted with a deepening economic crisis. He had to draw on loan money just to pay the ordinary expenses of government.

I observed earlier that Lyons' personal experiences as a child had a profound impact on his attitudes. From an early age, he learnt that hard work and education were keys to success. Just as Allan Martin would conclude that Robert Menzies did not lust after wealth, the same judgment could be made of Lyons. When he was opposition leader in the early twenties, Enid wrote of severe privation for the family, with a growing number of children – she was then pregnant with their fifth child – and much of his salary being spent on electoral obligations, such as travel and support for various constituents.

The personal and the public merged when Lyons became Premier in 1923. Lyons' campaign on deficits and debt, and the stagnating population, had been gaining traction in the previous few years, leading even to the normally hostile Hobart *Mercury* expressing disenchantment with the ailing Nationalist government of William Lee. When Lee lost a vote in the Assembly, the Lieutenant Governor, Sir Herbert Nicholls, rejected advice to call an election and called on Lyons to form a ministry, resulting in a minority government supported by a number of Nationalist Party members.

It was a mark of faith in Lyons by Nicholls, who as Chief Justice during the War had made sectarian remarks about Lyons' Catholicism. As subsequent events illustrated, Joe Lyons had the ability to look beyond the barbs of public debate, possessed a genial personality and a preparedness to bring otherwise divergent individuals together in pursuit of a common cause. This he had achieved in the Labor Party after the disastrous 1922 election failure. Clear purpose and a conciliatory approach became the hallmark of Lyons in government.

Although Lyons had adopted the rhetoric of socialism in his early political years, his approach was pragmatic. His wife, Enid, later recalled that both Joe and she felt uneasy about Labor's adoption of the 'Socialist objective' in 1921. On conscription, he agreed with Mannix (although for different reasons); on state aid to Catholic schools, he took a contrary view. He viewed his role as a representative of the people, albeit formed by a clear set of values. At a time when religious differences were strong, Lyons retained friends of all denominations. His marriage to Enid Burnell was an example.

The story of Joseph Lyons is incomplete without reference to the remarkable partnership with his wife Enid, whose contribution to public leadership deserves a separate lecture. When they married at St Brigid's Catholic Church, Wynard three days after the ANZACs had landed at Gallipoli in 1915, Joe was the Treasurer and Education Minister, and Enid a student teacher. He was 35 and she 17. The couple had to negotiate the religious antipathies of the day. Some members of Enid's devout Methodist congregation objected to her marrying a Catholic. It appears that Lyons hoped that she would convert, writing to her at one stage 'I shall fervently pray that the kindly light that led Newman will lead you too,' a reference to the journey from Anglicanism to Catholicism of the man after whom this college is named. After considerable soul-searching, Enid made a similar journey.

Enid Lyons lived an extraordinary life. The mother of 12 children, a collaborator with Joe during his public life, and the first woman elected to the House of Representatives and the first female to serve in an Australian cabinet is the merest summary of her achievements.

There were many pressures on the family. Their financial situation was often challenging; Enid had a number of miscarriages and suffered periods of depression. They often moved residence, living at various times in Devonport, Deloraine, Hobart – and subsequently in Melbourne and Canberra where they were the first family to live The Lodge. Travel was long and arduous: 9-12 hours from Hobart to the north-west coast by train, subsequent ferry crossings of Bass Straight by boat, and longer train journeys to Canberra and elsewhere around Australia. Enid recalled a school excursion from Burnie to Launceston, a 100 mile journey that took 6 hours by train.

At times the family was split and Joe and Enid often spent lonely times apart. In 1926, Joe nearly died when the car in which he was traveling crashed with a train, killing the then Speaker of the House, and leaving Joe hospitalized and in rehabilitation for months learning to walk again.

Enid often travelled with her husband, speaking on tours to the extent that critics at the time and since have suggested that he was essentially her puppet. In her memoir, *Among the Carrion Crows,* Enid rejected this and other put-downs of Joe:

> We leaned upon each other in an equality of partnership in marriage rarely achieved, even though we shared no common background. In upbringing, we were as far apart as the poles. When our views coincided it was, as often as not, the result of long discussion. When they differed, we were content to argue good-humouredly for years. We read together and laughed together. We shared our dreams and sometimes our labours. But that I was privy to all his political decisions, prompter of his political actions, adviser on every political problem is simply not true. Neither my public activities, my family responsibilities nor the state of my health would have permitted it. Nor, indeed, would it have been tolerated by his Cabinet or by his own independent mind.

If we need a reminder that there are constants in Commonwealth-State relations, consider the situation in the 1920s. Both Tasmania and Western

Australia were complaining about their inadequate share of Commonwealth revenue. Lyons, as Premier and Treasurer, responded with tough measures, raising taxes; curbing public service expenditure; appointing a Tasmanian Developmental Advisory Board and including leading industrialists amongst its members; and making a concerted approach to the Commonwealth for a better deal for the State.

The approach displayed Lyons' ability to bring diverse individuals and groups together. It would have been easy for the new Premier to blame the previous Nationalist Party administration, although Premier Lee had worked to attract investment – especially in zinc smelting – in efforts to promote economic activity. Instead, Lyons brought the Nationalists on board, including them in the drafting of a memorandum to the Commonwealth, and subsequently including all Tasmanian federal MPs in his meeting with acting Prime Minister Earle Page, at which he finally won concessions for the State.

In his doctoral thesis on Lyons, JA Hart summarizes the achievements of Lyons within his first two years in office:

> Taxation was reduced and more equitably imposed, loan expenditure reduced, all public service salary cuts restored, and the State's Shipping Line, established with Labor's approval in 1920 to provide

> transport to the mainland, was hastily sold, as it had proved an expensive liability. Although expenditure increased, the state of the economy improved, and in 1925 Lyons produced the first budgetary surplus for years.

This was the first glimmer of hope for the State, but there were many more challenges. The debt was still significant, economic activity was uneven, there remained significant areas of high unemployment and the Legislative Council, the upper house, had used its powers to block money bills. Noting a split in the Nationalists and knowing, as it was subsequently revealed, that the previously antagonistic Lieutenant Governor Nicholls opposed the blocking powers of the Council, Lyons sought - and ultimately gained - Royal Assent for the Appropriation Bill passed by the Assembly, but rejected by the Council. Even the conservative *Mercury* congratulated Lyons, although it did later question the process by which the outcome had been achieved.

Lyons' popularity soared. Previous suspicions about him in conservative quarters waned. In parallels with the Hawke-Keating approach decades later, Lyons addressed his challenges realistically and honestly, reached out to industry, and increasingly moved to the centre ground of politics. The apogee of this approach came in his successful 1925 election at which Labor was returned with a narrow majority. Opening his campaign at Deloraine, Lyons spoke as a Tasmanian Premier, not a Labor leader. He subsequently rejected criticism from his own supporters for not pursuing aspects of Labor's social agenda by explaining that it was what he promised in that campaign speech, not the platform determined by the Labor Executive, that constituted his program for government. Launceston's newspaper, *The Examiner*, proclaimed that Lyons had not offered Labor policy and was flummoxed by his promise, as a Labor leader, to encourage capital to the state.

Like his counterpart, Ted Theodore in Queensland, Lyons had faced adversity, outmanoeuvred his opponents and transformed Labor from a divided and distrusted group of 'socialists' into a party intent on governing for the mainstream. This has been a repeated lesson in Australian politics.

Politics is a fickle pursuit, as Lyons soon discovered. Some questionable business activities led to the resignation of his deputy, Albert Ogilvie, and bitterness within the government. Unions were agitating for industrial protections that were rejected by the Legislative Council, and the conservatives under John McPhee, whom Lyons personally admired, were on the rise. At the first election with compulsory voting in Tasmania, Labor commanded a majority of votes, but failed to win enough seats to form government. Rather than cling to government with the support of an independent, Lyons chose opposition. Anne Henderson observed:

> Lyons had moved well beyond simply being a Labor leader to something akin to chairman of the board managing the state. But this very unique Lyons style did not, at this point, serve him well in a Westminster system of politics, whatever it might have achieved in the best interests of the state.

The Westminster system is unique in the demands it places on leaders. Not only do they have to be able to effectively campaign from opposition to win office, and unify colleagues with often-competing interests and aspirations, but also transition from opposing to governing, or from being a minister to a leader. Not all have these abilities.

Lyons' regard and support was such that he remained leader after the election loss, but there were signs that his interest in state politics was waning. The family was back at Devonport where Enid, then 31, gave birth to their ninth child who suffered from dwarfism. In a period that Enid later described as 'The Golden Year,' Joe travelled less and spent more time with the family. But he also needed to support the family financially, and for the second time, went into business to supplement his Parliamentary income.

The social security measures we take for granted were still more than a decade away – family allowances did not exist. The national Labor leader, James Scullin, tried to entice Lyons into the federal ranks in 1928, but was rebuffed. It may well be that neither Joe nor Enid were enthusiastic about the thought of the long travels and separation involved in serving in the national Parliament, which had just moved from Melbourne to Canberra. Enid later wrote:

> For myself and the children I long to say No, for Joe I wanted to say Yes. . . But my mind always turned to the future – to the long separations . . . the distances that would divide us and to continuing insecurity.

# 4

# Turbulent Times

A year later in 1929, Joseph Lyons made the long journey to Canberra, after winning the Federal seat of Wilmot at the snap October House election at which the Bruce-Page administration was defeated, and Prime Minister Bruce lost his seat of Flinders. Scullin, who had been elected leader of the Labor Party in 1928, invited the former Premier to become Postmaster-General in his new government, taking a position in the Cabinet alongside another former Premier, Queensland's Ted Theodore. It was the beginning of a turbulent period as the economy faltered.

Canberra in 1929 was in embryonic form. A few major structures – the temporary Parliament House, the Melbourne and Sydney shopping buildings, the Canberra, Ainslie and Kurrajong Hotels, and the Lodge each stood in surrounding fields and parklands where sheep and cattle grazed. The Commemoration

Stone at the Australian War Memorial was unveiled on ANZAC Day that year. It would be three decades before the centrepiece of Walter Burley Griffin and Marian Mahony's grand plan for the national capital, a lake on the Molongo River, would be constructed. The great departments of State and the High Court were still located elsewhere, mainly Melbourne and Sydney. Rather than a town, Canberra was a collection of small, separated settlements. Upon first visiting, Enid Lyons described it as 'a strange place in a strange setting.'

The journey to the new national capital was by train from Melbourne or Sydney via Goulburn. Air transport was still in its early days – Bert Hinkler had completed the first solo flight from England in 1928, while Charles Kingsford Smith and Charles Ulm had flown from America. They were to form a new airline, the Australian National Airways Ltd, just a few years after the Queensland and Northern Territory Aerial Service (QANTAS) commenced operations at Winton in Queensland. Future Prime Minister, Joseph Lyons, was to become one of the most avid users of this new form of transport as he criss-crossed the nation like no leader beforehand.

The first transmission from the National Broadcasting Company was made from the 3LO studios in Melbourne in 1929; Hoyts was converting its theatres from 'silent' to 'talkie' pictures; and an early prototype of the television was first demonstrated. England had retained the ashes at the MCG while Collingwood won the third of four successive premierships. Owen Dixon was appointed to the High Court. Robert James Lee Hawke was born at Bordertown, South Australia; and John Douglas Anthony, a future National Party leader, whose father was to be elected to the House of Representatives in 1937, was born at Murwillumbah in northern New South Wales.

When Joe and Enid journeyed to Canberra, Enid had only recently given birth to their tenth child, Rosemary. Enid recalled in *So We Take Comfort* that:

> Burnie [where she was awaiting the birth] was outside the electorate of Wilmot, so I could not expect to see him while [the campaign] lasted, but on the day my baby was born he made a flying trip by train to visit me and welcome his new daughter. He was with me only an hour.

The pattern of separation, which Enid had already experienced in Tasmania, was to continue as Joe threw himself into his new federal ministry. Even today, with rapid transport and instantaneous communications, the life of a federal Parliamentary spouse is demanding as she or he is often left to raise family alone while her or his partner is in Canberra, elsewhere around the nation, or at the many events and functions in the electorate. How much more so eight decades ago? Enid wrote of the campaign:

> I was certain that Labor would win. I believed that Joe would also, but something within me that I could not stifle still pleaded against success and all the disruption of our lives that it would entail.

That disruption included moving the family to Melbourne where the Postmaster-General's offices were located before moving back to Devonport a year later when Joe became the acting Treasurer.

Economic and political storm clouds were already gathering on the horizon when Lyons was sworn into the Australian Parliament. The new Scullin government was confronted with a deteriorating financial crisis. For a decade, the Commonwealth and State governments had been reliant on overseas loans. The accumulated deficit was about 12 per cent of the Commonwealth's revenue. Commodity prices were falling and unemployment growing at an alarming rate. UK credit was becoming more difficult to obtain, as banks in the old country gave preference to domestic requirements. Australia was already in a significant slump before the 1929 stock market crash that signalled the Great Depression. The nation faced the perfect storm of crippling debts compounded by a global credit crisis.

As Douglas Copland spelt out in his 1933 Alfred Marshall Lectures at Cambridge University, two of the pillars of the 'Australian Settlement', namely industry protection and a rigid industrial relations system, were already failing the nation. As the 1929 Tariff Inquiry revealed, high tariffs retarded export growth and increased prices. The Brigden Committee observed that 'the tariff has probably reached the economic limits and an increase ... might threaten the standard of living.' Its call for more moderate tariffs fell on deaf ears, as the Scullin government increased income and indirect taxes and introduced higher rates on some 200 items on the tariff schedule, hoping that Australians would buy more locally produced goods. Immigration programmes were also suspended as unemployment ballooned towards 20 per cent. Strikes lasting for months at a time occurred, contributing to an already faltering economy.

By early 1930, the chairman of the Commonwealth Bank warned that it would be difficult just to meet the funds required to support the nation's debt and interest payments, leaving no funds for any other purpose. The nation was in a dire situation as national income fell from £640 million to £560 million.

While Scullin, Theodore and Lyons – the leaders of the Commonwealth government – believed that the nation was living beyond its means and savings had to be made, other voices, particularly in New South Wales, were advocating credit expansion. The political storm clouds were gathering above the Scullin government, with its large caucus, including a significant number of members who were baying for the opportunity to rebalance – in their perception – the role of labour and capital. Political events in New South Wales, the most indebted jurisdiction in the Commonwealth, were to aggravate the already difficult situation.

At the 1929 national elections, New South Wales swung significantly to Labor, with almost half of the new caucus from the state. The state election the following year of the Lang government created an explosive situation. Jack Lang, who had been Premier from 1925 to 1927, when he lost to the Nationalists, was an imposing figure. Manning Clark, who had praised the first administration of Lang, was caustic in his assessment of the 'Big Fella's' return in his *A Short History of Australia*:

> Somewhere between his first assumption of office in 1925 and the state elections in the middle of 1930 . . . he became corrupted by the power he wielded within the party. He began to demand blind obedience to his will . . . He became a demagogue; street hoardings proclaimed 'Lang is right', or 'Lang is greater than Lenin'; at huge public meetings in

the Sydney Domain crowds cheered to the echo as
he ranted against the English bondholder.

Lang was becoming one of the most destructive forces in Australian politics as his increasingly populous rant against the banks was taken up by many in the Labor caucus. Although Scullin, Deputy Prime Minister Jim Fenton, Lyons and – at that stage – Treasurer Ted Theodore had steadfastly rejected credit expansion and insisted that the nation had to pursue savings, including the reluctant decision to reduce wages and lay-off public servants, the rampant Lang presented a new threat as he railed against the banks and called for the repudiation of the nation's loans.

Australia had already acquired a very poor reputation in London, then as now, the financial capital of the world. As early as 1924, John Maynard Keynes used Australia – New South Wales in particular – to argue that the Dominions were able to borrow 'too cheaply resources which we [the UK] can ill spare.' That warning went unheeded. By the end of the decade, Australia's debt binge was exacerbated by the credit crisis of the Great Depression. It was a difficult situation for the new government, made worse by the political infighting by Lang and his supporters in the federal caucus.

In what would be considered unthinkable today,

Prime Minister Scullin, who had been ill, was out of the country for five months in 1930, attending the Imperial Conference in London. Ted Theodore was also sidelined while an investigation occurred into the collapse of a mine in which the Queensland government had invested while he was Premier of the northern state. In the absence of Scullin and Theodore, Jim Fenton was the Acting Prime Minister, and Lyons became the Acting Treasurer. The Imperial Conference was important – it finalised what became known as the *Statute of Westminster* which established the legislative independence of the self-governing dominions such as Australia – but Scullin's absence from Australia allowed his opponents within Labor to destabilise the party.

One of them, Frank Anstey, the Member for Bourke, then centred on the Melbourne suburb of Brunswick, was a radical socialist whose writings and statements revealed a conspiratorial dislike for capital and a fervent anti-Semitic distrust of bankers. He believed that Robert Gibson, the head of the Commonwealth Bank, and upon whose advice the Scullin government relied, was a supporter of the Nationalist Party and hostile to Labor. The Labor Party was fragmenting just as Scullin and Lyons were trying desperately to save the nation from even greater economic disaster. Something had to give.

The 1930 visit to Australia by Sir Otto Niemeyer, a representative of the London financiers, was the catalyst for the dramatic events which followed in 1931. His apparent disdain for the colonials did not help Niemeyer's cause in Australia, nor did the often – although incorrect – anti-Semitic attacks on him in the left-wing press of the day, and by radicals such as Jack Lang and Frank Anstey. For Scullin and Lyons, who knew that Australia would require more loans in the future to avoid bankruptcy, his message to the Premiers' Conference in Melbourne to balance budgets and reduce national indebtedness was reassuring. At the end of the meeting, a so-called 'Melbourne Agreement' was made in which governments decided to end borrowing and balance their accounts. The announcement had a positive impact in London, but it was already being attacked at home. A conference of unions and the ALP in Sydney rejected the approach, called for a moratorium on interest payments, the repudiation of war debts, and immediate financial stimulus for the economy.

Lang and his supporters in the Federal Cabinet called for the repudiation of the Melbourne Agreement and credit expansion in the face of the request by Fenton and Lyons to put the measures to the Parliament for approval. Open warfare had broken out in Cabinet and caucus. The radicals were in the ascendency and carried a motion at a marathon four-day caucus meeting to force the Commonwealth Bank to take up a £28 million loan falling due in December.

As the nation waited with bated breath, the 40 members of the Labor caucus met from morning until late into the evening over four days in Canberra. Their Prime Minister, Jim Scullin, was in England. Buoyed by the success of Jack Lang in New South Wales, the radicals were in no mood for compromise. Even after hearing from Lyons at length about the dire financial situation of the nation and the Niemeyer advice, they moved a motion to reject it. This was a crisis in Australian politics never experienced before. On the second day, a motion was moved to force the Commonwealth Bank to take up the £28 million loan falling due in December, to which Lyons moved an amendment to reassert government policy. Even Ted Theodore – who had returned to Parliament, and was locked in a battle with Lang for the control of the NSW Labor Party – had abandoned his earlier support for savings.

By the third day, the caucus rejected the position being put by Lyons, who had emerged as the *de facto* leader of the government in the absence of Scullin. Undaunted, Lyons cabled Scullin in London, whose reply he read to the caucus the next morning: Scullin supported his Acting Treasurer, stating that the caucus decision would lead to the withdrawal of money from Australia. The radicals were unrepentant. John Curtin proposed that the Ministry meet with the Commonwealth Bank directors to instruct them to take up the £28 million loan or resign, and Anstey proposed a bill be passed by Parliament to renew the loan for a year. The motions were passed, although Theodore did not support the latter, believing that it would kill any confidence in the financial affairs of Australia overseas.

When the meeting finished on the evening of the fourth day, the view of Lyons and Fenton had been rejected. The caucus was willing to repudiate the nation's debt. Both he and Fenton announced that they would consider their position before Lyons boarded an overnight train to Melbourne. Frank Green, the Clerk of the House wrote in his memoirs, *Servant of the House,* that a Parliamentary colleague of Lyons, Albert Green, ran alongside the departing train at the Canberra station, shouting, 'For God's sake, don't do it Joe.'

A throng of reporters mobbed Lyons when he arrived in Melbourne the next morning for the transfer to the Tasmanian ferry. Having pondered his situation on the long restless trip from Canberra, Lyons announced that he would resign if Scullin supported the caucus decision. He had written to Enid about how 'blue' he felt as the burdens of office and the caucus revolt had worn him down. By the time he reached Devonport the following morning, the Prime Minister had responded by cable from London: Scullin rejected the caucus decision, and was fully supportive of his Acting Treasurer.

Joe Lyons had faced down the radicals. Had he not done so, with Scullin's support, Australia's economic future would have been very different. Scullin and Lyons were not unmindful to the human tragedy playing out across the nation, as total unemployment rose to around 20 per cent and dole queues lengthened by the day. But they believed that the repudiation of our debts, continued credit expansion and a refusal to make the necessary savings would have exposed even greater long term weaknesses in the national economy with a slower recovery from the Depression and ongoing social chaos.

Throughout those days of high political drama, and passionate debates, a certain propriety and decency was observed. The 1930s involved matters of great policy import. No-one moved to spill the ministry or replace the Prime Minister, who was away from the country for almost half of 1930 while these events played out – unlike recent years when Prime Ministers have been dispatched because of poor polls. Yet, by the time Scullin returned to Australia in early 1931, his government was being torn apart internally.

Lyons' rejection of debt repudiation was rewarded in December when the loans fell due. Even though the bonds offered a lower interest rate and return, the offer was oversubscribed following appeals to patriotism by Lyons and a concerted campaign by the major newspapers. The appeal was bipartisan, with State premiers (except Lang) and major business leaders joining with Lyons to promote the need for the conversion of the loans as a matter of national interest. Increasingly Lyons was seen as a potential national leader who could unite various individuals and their different interests. A small group, that included the stockbroker Staniforth Ricketson and a young Victorian state MP, Robert Menzies, coalesced around Lyons. It included a former editor of *The Age*, Ambrose Pratt, and Keith Murdoch, father of Rupert.

Lyons' success was short-lived as forces of destruction engulfed the Scullin government. Intrigue replaced policy-making, as at least three different factions emerged. Ted Theodore was angling to replace Scullin, adopting a position on the debt that appeared contrary to his earlier statements and which was at least ambiguous. Further manoeuvrings came to a head at a caucus meeting on Australia Day 1931 at which Scullin retained the Prime Ministership, but Theodore was reinstated as Treasurer. Believing they had been betrayed by Scullin, Fenton and Lyons resigned from the ministry. Open warfare broke out in the New South Wales Labor Party: it would not be long before the Australian government imploded.

Lyons remained convinced that the new direction of the government, in which Theodore proposed an £18 million credit expansion, would be disastrous for the nation. He was censured at the Tasmanian Labor conference in late February, despite having been a successful State Premier and Federal Treasurer. The media began to speculate that he would leave the Labor Party, as the Senate rejected Theodore's plan. The Ricketson group in Melbourne was courting Lyons, but he was still pondering the best course of action. In her portrait of Enid in *Prime Ministers' Wives*, Diane Langmore writes:

> With her profound faith in the probity and ability of her husband, she [Enid] believed these goals [of equity, security and justice] could be best achieved by abandoning the paralysed Labor Party. Without her conviction Joe might never have made the break.

Things came to a head on March 13, 1931, when Lyons rose to his feet in the House of Representatives to speak on a 'Want of Confidence' motion in the government. The debate had lasted a number of days and Lyons was one of the last to contribute. It was to be his final speech as a member of the Labor Party, and one of the most powerful spoken in the people's chamber:

> I realize that my position today is a serious one. In recording my vote on this motion I shall be taking a stand which, according to the rules of the Federal Executive of the Australian Labor party, will automatically place me outside my party. I realize that the effect of that will be to separate me politically from men for whom, since I have been in this Parliament, I have developed a real affection and respect, men who have not only been colleagues, but comrades in the truest sense of the word.

Lyons went on to argue why the policy of credit expansion and inflation would increase unemployment, misery and destitution. He stated that he had lost confidence in Scullin, not in his personal integrity, but in his leadership, probably a reference to the pressures upon him from the Langites, but more so Theodore. The subsequent release of secret cables between Scullin and Lyons, which provided clear evidence that Lyons had faithfully supported his Prime Minister's advice from London, illustrated the extent to which Lyons chose not to highlight what he considered a betrayal by his own leader. He condemned the Federal Labor Executive as a body not responsible to the people, not the last time that such a charge would be laid. And he repeated the firm position that he was committed to advancing: 'We must put our house in order. I know that it is unpopular to talk about cutting down expenses, but we have to do it.' And in an indictment that resonates down the decades, he castigated those who would defend the salary and wages of the employed while ignoring those with no such emoluments – the unemployed.

It was Joe Lyons' farewell to Labor. He had flirted with the idea of quitting politics entirely, but abandoned this thought, possibly because of his need to provide for a wife and large family, as much as any other consideration. Ultimately, it was a matter of principle, neither feigned nor imaginary. He had remained loyal to the very end, and ultimately did what he considered the only honourable thing. In an era in which leadership is something determined by the polls, it is worth reflecting on the honourable position taken by Lyons. As Frank Green, the Clerk of the House for almost 20 years wrote, 'Lyons did not leave Labor of his own volition; he was driven out.'

Lyons crossed the floor with four colleagues. A fifth joined them soon afterwards. The government survived the 'Want of Confidence' motion by a handful of votes, but it was only a matter of time before the destructive Lang faction abandoned Scullin and effectively brought down the government.

Surprisingly, the Scullin government staggered on for most of the year. When the Lang faction crossed the floor on November 25 to vote against a measure for the distribution of unemployment funds, the Prime Minister had no alternative but to advise the Governor-General, Sir Isaac Isaacs (the subject of the second lecture in this series) to dissolve Parliament and to issue writs for a General Election.

Volatility reigned throughout 1931. As the economic situation worsened, the government faltered under the pressure of internal divisions. Jack Lang, acting as if there was no depression, defaulted on the interest due to the Commonwealth on NSW loans. Various political movements were springing up in the community and attracting large followings. At least 200,000 people – probably twice that number – had joined political movements such as the increasingly powerful All for Australia League. To put this in context, less than 100,000 people are members of political parties in Australia today when the population is almost fourfold what it was is the 1930s.

For some time, it appeared that Lyons might form his own party, as he and Enid addressed large rallies around Australia. It was during these rallies that Enid's role as a speaker blossomed. She particularly appealed to women, making the pair a formidable team. At

Ballarat she captivated the audience in repeating what Joe had said to her after the split:

> We have no money... But we have got the children. ... And by heavens, no one is going to spoil this country for them as long as I can lift a finger to stop it.

Powerful figures, including Keith Murdoch and Robert Menzies, increasingly saw Lyons as the solution to the malaise into which the nation had fallen. He remained cautious. The popular movements had blossomed in the absence of effective political leadership and a concern about the financial direction of the nation. They were often better organised than the existing political parties, but had only nebulous plans. Lyons' ability to negotiate his way through the confusing and often clashing agendas and interests was a mark of his quiet ability to manage adversity. Nor was it plain sailing in the Nationalist Party, led then by John Latham. Lyons was not prepared to force Latham from the leadership, knowing well that many in the Nationalists had difficulty in accepting a former Labor figure, and some were openly hostile. Equally there were some who followed Lyons from Labor, but could not take the further step of a marriage with the Nationalists.

Latham reluctantly stood down as leader in favour of Lyons in April, paving the way for the formation of a new party – the United Australia Party. The tens of thousands of Australians who were members of the various conservative movements that had sprung-up during the depression, many of them former Labor supporters, became the base of the new party.

As the Labor government of James Scullin clung to power, Ted Theodore, the Treasurer, was locked into a futile attempt to pass his fiduciary note issue bill through the Senate, a proposal that was finally rejected by the upper house on April 17. To employ a recently coined expression, the Scullin government 'was in office, but not in power'. Lyons was formally elected leader of the UAP on May 7, leading to bitter debates in the House as the new party moved a 'Want of Confidence' motion in the Scullin Labor government. The raw political tensions that had bubbled just below the surface now erupted in the chamber and across the nation. One of Lyons' former Labor colleagues, George Gibbons, accused 'reactionary forces and commercial institutions' of ''sucking the vitality and lifeblood out of the workers, and endeavouring to destroy those organisation through which they have secured the only power they now possess.' If anyone thinks that debates in the national Parliament are more spiteful than ever, a reading of *Hansard* from the era will reveal deep bitterness and division, as Joe Lyons joined Billy Hughes in the netherworld of Labor rats.

The various parties to the mounting conflict were playing for high stakes. When Lang refused to pay the interest on loans due to the Commonwealth, Scullin and Theodore responded by reducing payments to New South Wales by the default amount. While clinging to a faint hope that his legislation would pass the Senate, Theodore was already at loggerheads with the Commonwealth Bank. When its chairman, Robert Gibson, informed the Treasurer, who was also Chairman of the Loan Council, that it could no longer provide financial assistance to Commonwealth or State governments, Theodore angrily replied that the government would tell the bank what to do, not vice versa.

As Anne Henderson concludes:

> [Gibson] did not waiver in his belief that Australia could not afford to inflate the nation's costs or devalue its currency in the face of steep overseas interest repayments and tight international credit. Debt could not be brought under control by more debt – and Australia was too small a player in financial markets to stand alone or repudiate.

It was against this background that the Premiers' Conference was convened at the Victorian Parliament House on May 25. By contrast to Premiers Conferences these days which barely last three hours, the 1931 meeting went for three weeks! At issue was a proposal to convert an enormous £500 million loan by forcing bondholders to accept a significant reduction in the interest rate. The opposition leaders, Lyons and Latham, who were invited to the Conference for the third week by a weakened Scullin, opposed the compulsion, leading to a compromise provision whereby the offer was voluntary, but could ultimately be forced on bondholders. Although Lyons accepted the compromise plan at first, he later spoke against it, as overseas investors baulked and small bondholders protested the loss of their savings. With the Langites preparing to move against Scullin, the government's days were numbered. The end finally came on November 25 when the Lang faction crossed the floor to vote against their own Labor Prime Minister.

The December 19 election was a disaster for Labor. The primary vote plunged from 49 per cent in 1929 to just 27 per cent. The United Australia Party won three-quarters of the House seats, a bigger swing than Malcolm Fraser's landslide in 1975. Theodore lost his seat, and Labor would not occupy the Treasury benches for a decade. The age of Lyons had arrived. He had criss-crossed the country during the election at a pace that even some subsequent campaigns have not matched.

The dramatic events of the early 1930s illustrate that few things are immutable in the political landscape. In the end, hundreds of thousands of ordinary Australians chose to follow a plain-speaking leader who had a plan and was prepared to make hard decisions, even if unpopular, rather than reward a disunited government. Many of them voted for a party other than Labor for the first time.

# 5

# Saving the Nation

Lyons faced formidable challenges on coming to office. The outstanding public debt of all levels of government in Australia had grown from 127 per cent of GDP in 1929 to 205 per cent in 1932. Unemployment reached almost 20 per cent of all workers (to use the most accurate current measure). The Great Depression ravaged the world. Lyons had managed to unite disparate political forces. He may have lacked the oratory of Stanley Melbourne Bruce before him, or Robert Gordon Menzies later, but Lyons had qualities that helped him become the most popular Prime Minister since Federation. Long before John Howard coined the expression 'the broad church', Lyons was governing from the pragmatic centre. He clearly trusted his ministers to do their job until proven otherwise, perhaps overly so, and was a chairman of Cabinet in a style attributed to Bob

Hawke in the 1980s.

Lyons brought ex-Prime Minister Bruce back into the ministry, and later, Billy Hughes. Despite his dislike of small talk, Lyons had developed a genial public persona. He exploited new means of communications such as radio and the movie reel to great effect. He was the first Prime Minister that people connected with via the novel media of the era. He was also ably assisted by Enid, who was a major attraction in her own right. Photos of the couple, with their large family at the Lodge - the first family to reside in the home - were fodder for the newspapers and magazines of the time.

Lyons also knew the difference between opposition and governing. Undoubtedly his greatest achievements were to maintain a united team against improbable odds, and to quietly but firmly lead the nation from the precipice of economic ruin. He achieved the former by sustaining a conciliatory approach and the latter by firmly insisting on savings and the reduction of debts. Neither was easy to achieve.

In 1932, Jack Lang was in full flight in New South Wales, the most populous and economically significant state. At the Premiers' Conference in February, Lang announced that he would not pay any more interest to British bondholders. The Commonwealth had to step in with the payments, leading Lyons to declare that it would not make any more financial assistance available to New South Wales. As Lyons explained:

> Our unhappy financial position is largely due to the attempts of governments to provide employment on works constructed out of borrowed money, the interest of which has to be paid by the taxpayers of this country. Too many millions have in the past been expended on unproductive works which have robbed existing works of their reproductive capacity by coming into competition with them.

Following days of debate, the passage of the *Financial Agreement Enforcement Act* and the *Financial Agreement Act*, required banks to pay the Commonwealth moneys held or received by New South Wales. Lang responded by raiding the holdings of the Bank of New South Wales and the Commercial Bank of Sydney, and transferring the funds to the NSW Treasury. In the meantime, social chaos was threatening to explode into civilian turbulence and violence as Eric Campbell's New Guard and separatist movements exploited the turmoil. The events came to a dramatic head when a New Guardsman, Francis de Groot, charged across the about-to-be-opened Sydney Harbour Bridge on horseback, slashing the ribbon with his sword before Premier Lang could perform the ceremony. When the High Court rejected Lang's case against the Commonwealth Act, Lang instructed his departmental heads to ignore it, forcing the State Governor to sack Lang. Joseph Lyons' nemesis was wiped out at the subsequent NSW election, with Labor winning just 24 of the 90 seats.

The defeat of Lang secured political victory for Lyons, but the economic challenges remained. There is a thesis that Lyons achieved little during his years in office. Some – such as Lyons' colleague, Charles Hawker, who described his views as 'that of the man with small savings, [and] a home of his own' or the Labor newspaper *The World* comment that he was the victim of a suburban personality, 'an eminently well-meaning dullard' – seem motivated by partisanship. But others contended that there was little improvement in the economic malaise that afflicted the nation. These judgments will always be contested. It is a fact, for example, that total public debt in Australia in 1939 was still at 148 per cent of GDP. It is also true that little was done to reduce tariffs, even though leading economists were pointing to the stultifying impact of industry protection and a rigid arbitration system on productivity, growth and jobs.

It is important to judge the efforts of any individual or government against the constraints of the time, not some ideal determined decades later. By this measure, the available evidence suggests significant improvements in the Australian economy during the

1930s. The debt was brought down from 205 per cent of GDP to 148 per cent; unemployment fell from 20 to nine per cent and modest reforms of tariffs were made in a global environment which continued to support the existing trade system. Savings increased and there was no flight of capital. Writing in the *Sydney Morning Herald* in 1932, John Maynard Keynes supported Lyons' policies, concluding that they had 'saved the economic structure of Australia.' It is true that Keynes also believed that wage cuts were unnecessary as the nation had already been successful in the program of readjustment. If an international comparison is to be made, Australia climbed out of the Great Depression long before the United States, where unemployment rates remained stubbornly high and capital investment low right through the 1930s.

By his careful management of the United Australia Party, his attention to the interests and needs of business and workers, his extensive networking, and his ability to communicate his plans to the Australian people, Lyons created the length of time in government to achieve a great deal for Australia. While making the necessary adjustments required of any successful political leader, Joe Lyons remained committed to reducing debt, increasing savings, and creating trade opportunities for the nation. In 1932, he warned that the cost of pensions had blown out over the previous two decades and expenditure had to be contained. In 1935, the Cabinet was discussing trade opportunities with Japan; and on his overseas visits to the UK, the US and Canada, trade was a constant theme. While voices urging protection have been heard regularly in Australia, even today, a focus on opening up trade opportunities has been critical to our success globally. This outlook, and a focus on economic prudence, has been central to Australia's prosperity. Favourable Terms of Trade aided our growing prosperity in the mid-1930s, but reliance on high commodity prices always carries significant risks, as we have witnessed recently. In 1936, Lyons noted that Australia was still paying £25 million in interest payments to the UK, and faced ongoing economic challenges.

Efforts to obtain better trade deals for Australia in the 1930s had mixed success. After long negotiations more favourable arrangements for the export of beef to Britain were obtained. The flow of imports from the US to Australia concerned the Cabinet, as the corresponding export trade did not match. John Latham went to Indonesia, China and Japan to hold pioneering discussions about trade, but the ensuing conflict between Japan and China and concerns about Japanese expansionism ultimately muted these endeavours.

The lack of more progress on trade, particularly

with Japan, was linked also to Lyons' reliance on his Minister for Trade, Henry Gullett, who later resigned after being criticised by most of his Cabinet colleagues and various industry representatives. It was an illustration of where Lyons' more relaxed approach, especially to the work of his ministers, seems to have failed him and the government. My benchmark is Prime Minister John Howard with whom I served my longest period in Cabinet. Howard allowed his ministers to get on with their job, but was comprehensively briefed by his department on every issue, and regularly discussed matters in each portfolio with his Cabinet and backbench colleagues.

The outreach to Japan illustrated the shifting emphasis on foreign relations in Australia which was later confirmed in John Curtin's 'look to America' remarks in late 1941. A separate Department of External Affairs was created under Lyons, and the processes that led to the appointment of our first Ambassador in Washington commenced. Although a long-time pacifist, Lyons adopted a pragmatic approach to defence and security, as he did to most issues. With the horrors of the Great War still vivid, many leaders of the western world in the 1930s clamoured for peace, which culminated with the short lived Munich Agreement and the enthusiastic response to Neville Chamberlain's famous 'peace in our time' remarks. Winston Churchill was almost alone at the time in calling out the futility of appeasement. Lyons was steadily increasing military expenditure and the rearmament of our defence forces. Lyons, and his Treasurer, Richard Casey, pressed investment in technology and industrialisation as critical factors in national security.

Australia continued to regard its relationship with Britain as primary, but concerns about developments in our own region were mounting. Lyons floated a vague idea of a Pacific Non-Aggression Pact at the Imperial Conference in 1937, but the drums of war were already beating. Within two years, the world would be plunged into a global conflict, just two decades after the 'war to end all wars'.

Joe and Enid had long overseas visits in the mid to late 1930s, taking them away from family and nation for extended periods of time. They were together for weeks at a time, something absent from many years of political life, but Enid was often homesick and bored by many social functions. Writing in her diary after a reception at South Africa House, she commented: 'Of all the stupid crushes I ever attended it was the worst'; and of a 'stupid party' she attended with Lady Swaything: 'Stayed about twenty minutes – 19 ½ minutes too long.'

Lyons was feted on the world stage following his success in turning the Australian economy, a task that was greatly assisted by the work of Stanley Melbourne Bruce in assuring the London banks of the determination of the Australian government to redress financial problems.

Lyons' 1935 visit to England for the Silver Jubilee of George V was preceded by a visit to Ireland, the land of his ancestry. Lyons descended from families which supported the Irish Nationalist cause, but he was a supporter of the crown and empire. He took the principled Australian view against importing old enmities into the new country. This was reflected in his government's response the following year to the constitutional crisis precipitated by King Edward VIII in his determination to marry the American divorcee, Wallis Simpson.

Under the 1931 *Statute of Westminster* conventions (by which had Australia abided but had not formally ratified), the monarch required the consent of the Dominions to abdicate the throne, as he was king of each one. Given the marked change in social mores over the past century; it may be surprising today that the idea of the King marrying a divorcee with whom he had been having an affair, caused shock. But in 1936, the idea of the King, and head of the Church of England, marrying a twice-divorced woman was scandalous.

The British Prime Minister, Stanley Baldwin,

took it upon himself to consult the heads of the Dominions - Australia, Canada, Ireland, New Zealand and South Africa - about the matter. Baldwin advised the Dominions that the King hoped they would accept a morganatic marriage, but this did not find favour. Lyons advised Baldwin that his personal view was that 'the proposed marriage, if it led to Mrs Simpson becoming Queen, would involve widespread condemnation, and that the alternative proposal or something in the nature of a specially sanctioned morganatic marriage would run counter to the best popular conception of the Royal Family.' As Enid records *in So We Take Comfort,* Lyons had cabled the Private Secretary to the King, in which he:

> [E]xpressed the hope that His Majesty would give the fullest consideration to the vital fact that the Crown was the great unifying element in the British Empire and that any course calculated to weaken the ties of loyalty to the Crown or the position which it occupies in the affection and respect of the British people was fraught with danger to us all.

Lyons' concern for the unity of the British Empire can be contrasted with the approach taken by Ireland where the wily Éamon de Vallera, often referred to as the 'Irish Machiavelli', exploited the constitutional crisis to further establish independence from Britain.

De Vallera, like Lyons, an orthodox Catholic, responded that the Irish Free State had no 'personal' interest in the King. If however, opinions were sought, he was inclined to favour the King's choice of bride. Contrast this to the view of the man this lecture series honours, the Irish born and raised Daniel Mannix, who stressed that the proposed marriage would be unacceptable to His Majesty's Catholic subjects.

De Vallera recognized that abdication was the only alternative if the British people would not countenance divorce. On the day of the abdication, the Irish legislature passed the *Irish External Relations Act*, abolishing the office of Governor-General and limiting the Monarch's role to the appointment of diplomatic and consular representatives and the assent to international agreements on the advice of the Irish Government. De Vallera had clearly mastered the political advice to never waste the opportunity a crisis presents!

Lyons returned to Australia after the 1937 Imperial Conference and the coronation of George VI for a long and difficult election campaign against an energised Labor Party then led by John Curtin. Lyons repeatedly stressed that a strong and united Empire was necessary for world peace. In victory, he became the first Australian Prime Minister to win three consecutive elections. As we have witnessed in other periods of Australian politics, victory does not guarantee stability. Lyons' third term was difficult. Careful economic management remained vital while international tensions were rising. There was ongoing criticism from Labor supporters of Joe and his policies, including in the Catholic media. At one stage, he counselled Enid about the *Catholic Worker*, which had been founded by BA Santamaria:

> For Heaven's sake, don't worry about things like the Cath Worker etc. I used to worry dreadfully and it got me nowhere – only upset me and made me more miserable. Now I just either don't read them or say to myself, "You've done a pretty good job for Aust. And you can't work miracles.

Some thought that more should be done in preparation for possible conflict, although Joe's stress on the desirability of peace was widely shared amongst political leaders of the era. His government was also slow to respond to the growing exodus of Jews from Nazi Germany.

Within the UAP, succession was also an issue that inflamed tensions. For some time, Arch Parkhill, an influential organiser of the Nationalists in New South Wales, and a minister in Lyons' Cabinet, was viewed as an alternative to the Tasmanian. An impressive Parliamentary debater, Parkhill lost his seat of Warringah in 1937 to the conservative independent,

Percy Spender, who subsequently joined the UAP and became Minister for External Affairs and Ambassador to the US in the Menzies era.

Following his defeat of Jack Lang, the New South Wales Premier, Bertram Stevens, became a darling of many Nationalists who had a residual dislike of Lyons, the former Labor man. Stevens, however, over-reached at the Premiers Conference in 1938, advocating for a relaxation of the Commonwealth's credit policy, a call which led to a stinging put-down by Treasurer Richard Casey, perhaps Lyons' closest colleague despite their many differences.

That left the ambitious Robert Menzies, who had helped recruit Lyons to the leadership of the new UAP, and who would dominate the national stage after the Second World War. Menzies had good reason to hope that he would eventually become leader. As early as 1936, Lyons wrote to him saying:

> . . . for some time I have felt that the time had come for you to step into my shoes both because you should be given the opportunity to use your talents for Australia's benefit and because I feel that I have done a pretty good job . . . and I am entitled to a rest.

Menzies complained that Lyons was not doing enough, but he was biding his time; aware that his aloofness attracted criticism and that, first Parkhill, and then Stevens, were rivals. Although impatient, Menzies, it would seem, preferred Lyons to endorse him as his successor.

Menzies speech to the Constitution Club in Sydney after the Premiers Conference inflamed tensions in the government. The content of the *extempore* speech was never fully recorded, but it was perceived by Enid in particular as a direct attack on Lyons. Lyons and Menzies sought to downplay the interpretation, but damage was done. In *The Menzies Era*, John Howard wrote:

> Menzies' disavowal of any reflection, implied or otherwise, on the strength of Lyons' leadership was disingenuous.

Enid Lyons was in no doubt about Menzies' motives. Over thirty years later, she wrote in *Among the Carrion Crows:*

> For Menzies it was a continuing clash between desire and loyalty: the desire of a young ambitious man convinced of his own power to serve his country well, and the loyalty he owed to the Leader who had given years of selfless service, but whose capacity for further leadership he genuinely doubted.

Menzies subsequently resigned over the government's decision to abandon National Insurance legislation. Both Joe – who appears to have retained a belief in Menzies' integrity – and Enid, who seriously questioned it, viewed Menzies' resignation as the resolution of a problem that had been simmering for months. Menzies later wrote warmly of Lyons as the man 'who commanded my admiration and affection in an uncommon degree'.

In his biography of Menzies, Allan Martin suggests that Enid's response was protective of her husband and mindful that her own position and influence would cease if Joe was replaced. Enid appears to have buried any lingering resentment in an exchange of letters towards the end of their lives in which she accepted Menzies observation that 'two people looking at or participating in a series of events can quite honestly come out of the process with entirely different understandings on what had gone on.'

There was no move to replace Lyons. Paul Hasluck's observation was undoubtedly correct when he wrote:

> The pre-eminence of Lyons [was] due to the fact that he alone was respected and acceptable among a group of persons who did not all respect each other.

Joe was becoming weary of politics in the late 1930s. He had discussed retirement with Enid on the sea voyage back from London in 1937. In May 1938, he wrote to her:

> It is just dreadful to come back to what awaits me here [Canberra] but I suppose one day it will come to an end.

On another occasion, he wrote:

> I wish they would defeat us and we'd be out of our misery and get a little happiness.

Two weeks before Easter 1939, the couple decided when together at Devonport that he would retire, but he was pressured to stay on by leading Nationalist Party figures over the following Palm Sunday weekend in Melbourne. Days later, he suffered a major heart attack, dying with Enid by his side at St Vincent's Hospital, Sydney, on Good Friday. He was 59.

I will not to speculate on what might have happened if Lyons had lived on. It is clear that he was weary of politics and keen for someone else to take the reins, preferably Bruce. It is also the case that some previous supporters, such as Keith Murdoch, were moving to Menzies.

# 6

# Public Leadership

When Joe Lyons died, he left a widow and 12 children. There wasn't the social welfare or Parliamentary entitlements that exist today. Both Joe and Enid had given their lives to nation and family. The Parliament granted Enid an annuity which led to much bitter debate in the community. In an act of great generosity, Richard Casey and his wife, Maie, provided the funds so that Kevin Lyons could complete his schooling at Xavier College. Joe Lyons left an estate of just £344, although Enid owned the home at Devonport. He wasn't the only public figure of the era to leave office with little wealth. Lyons, Chifley, Curtin and Menzies did not view life and leadership as about financial and material rewards, but unselfish, indeed sacrificial, public service. Each also had a keen appreciation for the role of civil society. Australia is the richer for their contributions.

Dame Enid Lyons went on to forge her own further contribution to this nation. Diane Langmore writes:

> Of all the Australian prime ministers' wives, probably none stood more squarely beside her husband than Dame Enid Lyons. She achieved this position not only because of her own ability and willingness to do so but also because her husband sought an equality of partnership unusual for its time. She was Joseph Lyons ideal partner and he knew it.

No person who gains the keys to The Lodge is wanting in ambition, but in Joseph Lyons we had possibly our most reluctant Prime Minister; a man recruited to the role, who was prepared to leave it when others thought best, and who remained despite his desire to retire.

As Robert Menzies was to write in *Afternoon Light*:

> Lyons did not fall into the error of seeking to propound exciting new measures in a hurry. In spite of his uncommon talents, or perhaps because of them, he was essentially a man of the people. He understood ordinary men and women, and they understood him. He was a family man with many children. He was a comparatively poor man, with no silly social pretensions. The instinctive feeling he evoked from the public was that he could be trusted to do his best for the unfortunate,

> and for households grievously afflicted by the Depression . . . He succeeded in his task. In his own undemonstrative way, he illustrated the moral force of leadership.

Joe Lyons had a knack of drawing people together. He presided over a Cabinet with a very different background and experience to the school teacher from rural Tasmania. Three members of his talented Cabinet – Bruce, Hawker and Casey – were educated at Cambridge. Latham and Menzies had been leaders at the Bar. Three Cabinet members had been, or were to become, Prime Minister themselves.

In her masterful portrait of the great American president, Abraham Lincoln, Doris Kearns Goodwin describes how Lincoln reconciled conflicting personalities and forged a strong, united government from a team of rivals in challenging times.

Joe Lyons possessed a sanguine temperament in contrast to our era in which the extremely choleric has become the caricature of modern politics. He did not have to be the smartest person in the room. He was a facilitator and conciliator by nature and experience, working with other capable colleagues to achieve an objective. An ability to genuinely listen to the public and to colleagues is a mark of national leadership. As Václav Havel, the first president of the Czech Republic, reminded us:

> It is not true that only the unfeeling cynics, the vain, the brash, and the vulgar can succeed in politics: such people, it is true, are drawn to politics, but in the end, decorum and good taste will always count for more.

There is a sense that Lyons never picked a fight, but neither walked away from one when principle (or national prosperity) was at stake. Importantly, Enid's toughness and determination often plucked-up his resolve in the face of natural caution.

Good public leadership requires a genuine concern for the common good. But is also requires personal virtues, especially perseverance and courage. The character of a leader is exhibited in the face of adversity. A true leader must be prepared to plant a Standard in the ground and proclaim, 'Here I stand' – and, if necessary – 'Here I fall.' On our national debt and the imperative to save, Lyons stood firm. He had vision, a strategy and a constancy of purpose. He put the challenges confronting the Australian people before them and argued for a course of action, often in the face of populous opposition. Had he not done so, Australia would have been in a much weakened financial position at the outbreak of World War II.

Lyons provided a political bridge in Australian politics. Many workers first voted for a party other than Labor because of Joe Lyons' leadership of the

United Australia Party. The UAP also set the pattern for the Liberal Party which succeeded it, especially in the widespread involvement of many community groups and the representation of both conservative and liberal strands of political philosophy.

When he learnt of this lecture, Joe and Enid's eleventh child, Peter, now 84, wrote to me from Devonport. Reflecting on the fact that his father has virtually been neglected by history, he proffered two reasons:

> First the Parliamentary press – in fact most of the mainstream press of the country – is dominated by left wing thinkers and, to them, Dad was, and still is, regarded as a Labor Party rat. Second, Dad, who's Government was the United Australia Party, the forerunner of the Liberal Party, has never been totally embraced by the Liberals. And in any case the conservative side of politics generally does not lionise their Prime Ministers.

These lectures remind us of the significant contributions that have been made to the leadership of this nation long after people and events have passed.

Perhaps the final words can be left to Joseph Aloysius Lyons who in a letter to his wife and partner, Enid, wrote:

> Neither you nor I can put everything right and we

saved Australia from ruin. Think of the homes that are happy because of what we did and realise that no-one was unhappy because of what we did.

It is a fitting epitaph for a humble, generous man who led this nation through some of its most difficult challenges.

# Select Bibliography

Blainey, Geoffrey (1954) *The Peaks of Lyell* [Melbourne University Press, Melbourne]

Blainey, Geoffrey (1963) *The Rush that Never Ended* [Melbourne University Press, Melbourne]

Blainey, Geoffrey (2003) *Black Kettle and Full Moon* [Viking, Melbourne]

Brett, Judith (1992) *Robert Menzies' Forgotten People* [MacMillan, Sydney]

Clark, Manning (1963) *A Short History of Australia* [Mentor, New York]

Goodwin, Doris Kearns (2005) *Team of Rivals: The Political Genius of Abraham Lincoln* [Simon & Schuster, New York]

Green, Frank (1969) *Servant of the House* [Heinemann, Sydney]

Havel, Václav, Speech at New York University, October 27, 1991 in Paul Wilson (ed) (1995) *Václav Havel – Toward a Civil Society* [Lidové Noviny, Prague]

Henderson, Anne (2011) *Joseph Lyons – The People's Prime Minister* [New South, Sydney]

Henderson, Gerard (1994) *Menzies' Child* [Allen & Unwin, Sydney]

Howard, John (2014) *The Menzies Era* [Harper Collins, Sydney]

Kelly, Paul (1992) *The End of Certainty* [Allen & Unwin, Sydney]

Langmore, Diane (1992) *Prime Ministers' Wives* [McPhee Gribble, Ringwood]

Lyons, Enid (1965) *So We Take Comfort* [William Heinemann, London]

Lyons, Enid (1972) *Among the Carrion Crows* [Rigby, Adelaide]

Martin, A W (1993) *Robert Menzies – A Life* (Vol 1) [Melbourne University Press, Melbourne]

Menzies, Robert (1967) *Afternoon Light* [Cassell, Melbourne]

Nairn, Bede (1986) *The 'Big Fella'* [Melbourne University Press, Melbourne]

Ross, John (editor) (1993) *Chronicle of Australia* [Chronicle, Ringwood]

Santamaria, B A (1978) *Archbishop Mannix* [Melbourne University Press, Melbourne]

Shedvin, C B (1970) *Australia and the Great Depression* [Sydney University Press, Sydney]

www.ingramcontent.com/pod-product-compliance
Ingram Content Group UK Ltd.
Pitfield, Milton Keynes, MK11 3LW, UK
UKHW021257180426
11947UKWH00015B/887